FAMILY, NATURE, LOVE POEMS AND NEW BEGINNINGS

FAMILY, NATURE, LOVE POEMS AND NEW BEGINNINGS

ANGELICA OLIVER

Angelica Oliver
Family, Nature, Love Poems and New Beginnings

Published by Spines
ISBN 979-8-89383-452-9

DEDICATION

"I dedicate this book to Canaan, the love of my life and my most wonderful inspiration, who has guided me to reach for the stars."

CONTENTS

Part I
FAMILY, NATURE
Save   11

Part II
LOVE POEMS
It's a beautiful start to the day   67
Broken clouds   68
I gaze upon you   69
Sunny afternoon   70
When I'm with you   71
Thinking of you always   72
Clear morning   73
You captured my heart   74
Defenses down   75
Clouds are gray   76
My shining star   77
My true beginning   78
Loving you is easy to do   79
As the wind blows   80
My one and only   81
Sun shining brightly   82
The night is clear   83
The moon is shining   84
A raging storm   85
Thinking of you always   86

Part III
NEW BEGINNINGS
Beauty all around us   89

About the Author   179

PART I
FAMILY, NATURE

SAVE

The morning is bright with the sun shining overhead and the birds this morning are busy chattering, singing their beautiful melodies, and gathering food for the new ones in the nests. There was an early rainfall and the ground is still wet making it a tasty treat for the birds in search of fresh worms crawling around. With every new day, there's new love, fresh new promises to keep and new beginnings. Our world is always bustling around and sometimes it's hard to just take a moment to see how beautiful everything is around us. Birds are seen flying overhead and critters are scampering across the fields in search of new places to hunker down before the storm comes that's heard brewing in the distance yet again. A wonderful world to behold and cherish with each new day that is given to us.

Beautiful white flowers in bloom to grace my day

Nature is beautiful

Cloudy skies, but everything is beautiful still on the horizon. With love in my heart and the one by my side who I adore and cherish more than anything, another day is something to look forward to and I'm smiling as I embark on a new adventure. What discoveries will I find today? Each new day comes with the promise of something beautiful and something new to make memories from.

A wonderful morning with our feathered friends who grace us with beautiful songs.

Life is always full of surprises and we never know what's around the corner. It can be sad and heartbreaking or it can be wonderful and the best thing to ever happen to us. With every new day our world that we live in gives us those wonderful chances to experience and cherish love from one another. Whether it be the love of family, our furry friends, or someone who we want to share our life with and someone who stole our heart, life is beautiful and shouldn't ever be taken for granted because we never know when that last touch or kiss will be.

Darkened skies

Darkened skies and a gloomy start to the day, but in its own way it's beautiful. With the storm brewing on the horizon, it gives us that moment to think about how precious everything is and how things can be swept up and washed away only to make room for new life and beginnings. We should always cherish and hold close the ones who we love and care about in our lives because life is short. Like a rainstorm brewing and then washing everything away, life is that way too. Always hold on to what is precious and true to your heart.

Beautiful pink flowers to grace us this spring. Love and nature are intertwining this spring.

Flowers are blooming and there's beauty all around us. The warm air is blowing through the branches this morning and the sun can be seen on the horizon. It's a beautiful start to the day and everything seems clear. Walking along the flowering fields that surround me, I'm caught up in emotion when thinking about the one man in my life who swept me up and stole my heart away. To be in his arms again would be as beautiful as a warm sunny day. Gaze into my eyes and tell me how much you love me and let the wonders of our beautiful world around us take away our sorrows of yesterday.

The beautiful wonders of nature are all around us and we need to think about what's important in this world of ours that we share together because we might never get that one chance again. Furry friends abound in our lives and come to make our day bringing a much needed smile when we need that extra love. Let's love one another as things should be and always be on the lookout for that little critter just waiting to make our day.

Beautiful birds soaring the skies
Life is a mystery and full of twists and turns. Sometimes it can be scary and overwhelming to think about everything that could happen when you least expect it. With the love of someone close to you everything seems possible and not so scary. Life can be like a bed of roses, but can also feel like a bed of thorns too if we're not careful. Finding your special someone to share this world with is something wonderful and like life, love should never be taken granted of, but should be cherished and kept close to your heart.

Like a rose's thorns, life can be hard and painful, but like the beautiful and gentle flower pedals, life can also be beautiful and something to look forward to with each and every day. The struggles are real and we must pull ourselves up from the ashes and cherish who is close to your heart and who might be the one who lifts your spirits every day.

The world is in constant motion and it seems as though everyone is in a rush to get things done and to compete with the next one who rises above everyone else. Let time stand still for a moment and listen to the wind rustling through the branches on a cool, fall morning and watch as the waves come tumbling in on a hot, summer day. Life is short and just a glimpse in time. We're all here for just a short time and one needs to experience just how precious we all are and be there for one another.

Times are always changing and some things are as old as time like this old and weathered tree.

Sunlight is filtering through the branches this morning and a beautiful day is upon us again. I gaze up in awe at just how pretty the leaves and flowers are on the trees and wonder just how life can be so precious and beautiful to us. We take for granted things that are all around us and sometimes fail to really think about the wonders of nature that beckons us at every corner. Fresh, new life is growing as spring sets and colorful flowers sway in the breeze as the wind blows softly. A glimpse into everything beautiful as I walk along a wooded path and catch sight of a bird feeding her young up in a high nest above me. The sounds of beautiful chattering can be heard and I'm thinking about someone close to my heart as I stop and rest for a while. Life is but a beautiful thing to be able to share with someone and should always be cherished just like we cherish what nature puts before us every day.

The clouds are scattered across the sky and the sun can be seen trying to peek through on this beautiful spring day. What a wonderful site to behold and be able to listen as the seagulls cross over. They chatter as they go by and I'm caught up in thoughts of my love who captured my heart and who has given me the opportunity to feel everything new and beautiful again. To be free flying above the clouds with wings spread open is a glorious thing to see.

From the smallest critters to the biggest mammal on earth,
everything is precious.

Beautiful purple flowers
With each new season comes new growth and new experiences
for every part of life that is shared with us as we take this

voyage together through space on our small and beautiful planet we all call home. With the love of someone close we can see more clearly, experience things together and have that special someone to live out our life with as it unfolds. We all need to feel loved and to be able to experience some sort of closeness and companionship, for being alone is but a terrible thing to have to endure. Love one another and let someone know just how important they are in your life because you might never get that chance again. With having someone close, the seasons might change, but the love for one another will always remain.

Beautiful up high in the branches are our feathered friends My dreams came true when I met you, my most wonderful man in my life who has inspired me, loved me and motivated me to do things in life I never thought I could do. With each new season and every new year, I'm happier than words can ever say . Embrace me into your arms and we'll take this journey of life together and hope for beautiful things to come as every day unfolds. The future is bright with you by my side and as we walk along this tree lined cobble path, let's take in everything beautiful that we share together and look ahead to more wonderful experiences and memories that we create together. The sounds of a storm brewing can be heard off in the distance, the leaves are rustling as the wind picks up and as you hold me close you whisper " I love you" and kiss me upon my waiting lips.

Beautiful bumblebee resting for a bit on the windowsill. So beautiful, this tiny little creature who flew in to say hi. One of many of our precious lives that we have all around us every day. From just a tiny speck to the biggest thing that towers above us, everything has a purpose and is magical.

There's a beautiful moon out tonight
The beautiful moon lights a path for me to follow as I walk along the sandy seashore and I laugh as the cool waves rush up to take my breath away and my one and only wraps his strong arms around me. The air is light and warm as we make our way up the path to a sandy hillside to sit for a while and look at the twinkling stars above. It's always a beautiful sight to behold because every night is different and it can take my breath away

when I'm caught up in all the wonder that this world and my
love have to offer me.

A beautiful pink flower to bring a smile to your face
With every new day and every beautiful morning, I'm thankful
for finding the most wonderful man in my life and to be in your
arms forevermore would be like heaven to me. Love is a
beautiful thing to experience and my heart is on fire and I feel
like I'm floating above the clouds. I never knew that I would fall
this hard and that I could ever truly love someone as much as I
love you. You've shown me what true love can feel like and I
cherish everything that we share together. I'll always be there
for you. This I promise you. Loving you always.

Hanging out.

Cute bunny saying hello.

Pretty bird.

Pretty bird among the branches.

Looking down from above.

Flying over and on their way to the nest.

Checking things out.

A dog and his stick.

Time to snuggle.

Sitting pretty.

High up in the branches.

Bunny stopping for a quick visit.

Pretty bird this morning.

Happy boy.

Beautiful birds in flight.

On the wings of the bird flying over. A beautiful site.

Two of a pair enjoying the early morning.

Bunny on the run.

Spreading my wings.

Woodpecker capture.

Nap time.

Drying off after the rain.

A snowy morning and just hanging out for a bit.

Let's roll around in the snow.

Santa is coming and I've been a good boy.

Hanging out together.

A bug's life.

Slimy reptile saying hello.

Hopping on by.

The love of your best friend.

Me and my ball.

Munching away.

Beautiful bumblebee.

Beautiful butterfly.

Unique dragonfly.

Bunnies cuddling.

Hello there.

Beautiful pic of starfish on the beach.

Itty bitty baby bunny.

Resting here for a bit.

Ba humbug!

Funny story.

Yummy, that was good!

Fluffy bunny pic.

Creepy crawler.

I'll just hang out here for a minute.

What are you?

Jumping for joy!

Chilling.

On the lookout.

Me and my bone.

Just laying around.

Just being cute.

Chilling here.

Nap time.

Kitties exploring.

Geese on the move.

Vultures flying over.

Beautiful bird flying over.

Colorful bird.

Sitting pretty.

Beautiful bird up high in the branches.

Exploring.

Beautiful in nature.

High up in the clouds.

Up on the rooftop.

Perched on the post early in the morning.

Having fun out in the yard.

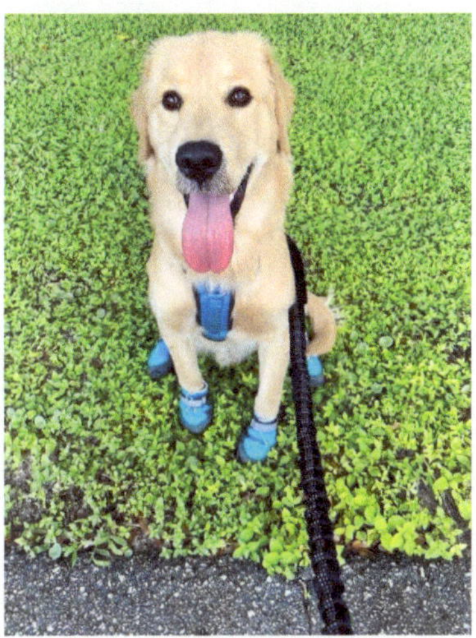

Me in my blue shoes.

Laying here for a bit.

In memory of my baby girl Bellah. My fur baby and the greatest dog who was my best friend.

PART II
LOVE POEMS

IT'S A BEAUTIFUL START TO THE DAY

It's a beautiful start to the day and all is calm.

The sun is filtering down through the swaying and flowering tree branches and the squirrels are happily chattering away while gathering nuts.

I'm caught up in images of the one man in my life who took my breath away and who continues to sweep me off of my feet.

I never would have imagined my life could be so beautiful as it is when we're together.

Show me the way to your heart, hold me close, kiss me deeply upon my waiting lips, and let's embrace till the morning comes once again.

You're my one and only, my dream come true and the one I've been searching for.

BROKEN CLOUDS

*B*roken clouds are scattered across the sky, but the sun is shining through and a smile crosses my face when thinking about you, my angel of mine.

With each day I love you more and I long for your closeness again.

I look out past the landscapes and thank God for another beautiful day and for giving me the chance to experience true love with the most wonderful man who was sent my way.

I never knew I would find my soulmate till I met you. Take me into your arms, hold me close and never let me go.

I GAZE UPON YOU

I gaze upon you and just watch as you sleep soundly.

You're dreaming of a beautiful world with a smile upon your lips.

Wanting to feel closer, I snuggle close and can feel the warmth of our bodies as we embrace together.

Softly, ever so softly, I kiss you on your parted lips.

You wake up groggily and I give you another kiss once more to catch a smile spreading across your face.

SUNNY AFTERNOON

It's a sunny afternoon and the birds can be heard up in the trees happily chattering away while the branches sway back and forth with the slight breeze blowing through.

Children's laughter can be heard too off in the distance and I'm thinking about peaceful moments spent with the man who lifted me off of my feet and stole my heart away.

As your fingers trailed through my hair you whispered I love you and my breath was taken away as we let time slip away with us as our bodies intertwined with each other and you kissed me ever so softly.

WHEN I'M WITH YOU

When I'm with you, the rest of the world seems to disappear.

I long for your warm embrace and sweet kisses. Loving you can only bring good things to pass.

You've brought me so much happiness and I'm blessed every day with you.

You coming into my life has set things in motion for a newer and better tomorrow.

My forever lies with you and I'll always cherish the moments that we share together.

THINKING OF YOU ALWAYS

Thinking of you always.

You came into my life and opened up my heart.

The thought of never finding you is incomprehensible.

I think about the future, being with you, and suddenly everything becomes clear.

Take my hand and lead me to your wonderful paradise because where you go I will follow.

You captured both my heart and soul and I love you.

CLEAR MORNING

The morning is clear and the sun is shining brightly.

A soft breeze is blowing through the branches and off in the distance the beautiful melody of a songbird can be heard.

Beauty surrounds us, but with everyday life, it can sometimes be hard to see.

We never know where life will lead us and what may be around the next corner, but to know that I have you is my greatest gift I could ask for.

Life may have its challenges, but to see your smile, see love in your eyes and to be in your arms again is everything I need to uplift my spirits and wipe all my troubles away.

A smile is forever on my lips with the love that I feel for you.

YOU CAPTURED MY HEART

ou've captured my heart, body, and soul with just one touch and one look from your mesmerizing eyes.

You've kindled my innermost desires and burning flame.

I'm not of myself anymore because I crave everything that you are and will be when we finally touch.

I long for you always and look forward to the day when our bodies become one.

My love, my destiny, you are forever with me in my heart.

DEFENSES DOWN

All of my defenses are down, my barriers broken, and my shattered soul on the mend once more.

True love and commitment I find in your trusting arms and tender kisses.

A cool breeze blows through as we gaze at each other longingly while walking hand in hand along the shore.

The sun is setting on the horizon and our embrace becomes closer as the day turns to night.

Once more, we look into each other's eyes and are drawn deeper into each other as we kiss.

The feelings of love are forever with us.

CLOUDS ARE GRAY

The clouds are gray this morning and are scattered across the cold and wintry sky.

The sun is hiding and birds can be seen flying overhead searching for their next meal.

It's a beautiful start to the day because I have love in my heart and I smile whenever I think about you.

I can't imagine a day without you, my sweet prince, because I found my true love in you and sharing my everyday life with you has given me more happiness than I've ever had.

You've lifted up my spirits and made every day that much more beautiful.

MY SHINING STAR

My shining star, my moon at night to light my way, you're my every breath that I take , a burst of fresh air, and a warm embrace that comes from loving you.

You're my inspiration and my reason to be able to look forward to the beautiful day that lays ahead.

Let's take each and every day that comes and cherish each new moment together.

MY TRUE BEGINNING

My true beginning and my never ending eternal love are always yours.

Nothing can ever compare to my feelings that I have for you, my love.

I come to you whole, open hearted, and bare to you my inner soul to have and to hold forever.

You've shown me your heart and your innermost self and I'll always cherish you.

True love knows no limits or boundaries. Mine is forever.

LOVING YOU IS EASY TO DO

*L*oving you is easy to do.

Everything is so fresh and new.

I cherish every day that I have with you and for making my moments not so blue.

You crossed my path and had me experience life in a wonderful new light.

Take my hand, hold me close, whisper sweet nothings in my ear and we'll share beautiful new memories together.

Always and forever yours.

AS THE WIND BLOWS

As the wind blows and raindrops hit the windowpane, my thoughts are of you and how beautiful life will be when we're together.

My love for you has grown and is surpassed to any other feelings I've ever known.

Words can't express how much I love you. In your arms, feeling the beat of your heart and tasting your sweet kisses as the rain falls steadily down outside is where I want to be.

Always loving you.

MY ONE AND ONLY

I found my one and only, my soulmate, my match to complete me, and my forever love to have now and for always.

You bring a smile to my lips when thinking about you and my heart is forever full of love because I have you in my life.

I weep happy tears with thoughts of seeing you and of holding you close.

My inspiration, my angel, you'll never know just how much I love you.

SUN SHINING BRIGHTLY

The sun is shining down brightly and there's a cool, crisp feeling in the air this morning.

The seasons will be changing soon and bring new experiences and memories to have and cherish.

I look forward to sharing many more beautiful moments with my one and only.

The angels above knew where our paths in life would lead us and I'm over the moon that my path led me to you.

With every day that goes by and every moment that we get to share together, my feelings for you just get stronger.

That first glance, first smile, first kiss, and the first time you took me to the stars has been everything to me and more than I could ever hope for.

Always loving you.

THE NIGHT IS CLEAR

The night is clear, there's a slight breeze blowing through and the moon is shining brightly down over the rippling waters.

A beautiful site to see while I'm laying here under the stars thinking of you.

You stole my heart with just one glance and stirred my soul and emotions in ways you'd never know.

My thoughts are forever of you and I fall weak when I'm in your arms.

My angel, I love you.

THE MOON IS SHINING

The moon is shining brightly lighting a path for me to follow and the wind whispers sweet nothings in my ear as I carefully make my way along the moonlit shore.

The stars above twinkle and shine down upon the calm waters off in the distance.

I skip along the sand and smile as my toes splash in the cool waves as the water comes rolling up onto the warm sand.

Dancing along the waters, I feel electrifying energy and I feel the cool waves rush up to meet me in a surprising blast that takes my breath away.

I take in the cool, salty air and make my way farther down the shore till I'm spent and breathless upon the sand with my angel beside me.

I gaze up in awe as you wrap your arms around me and I wonder how life can behold such beauty.

A RAGING STORM

Like a raging storm coming through, my love is forceful and strong wanting to make its way to you.

Loving you is the easiest thing to do and comes so naturally.

My love for you is true and never waivers.

My heart grows more love for you with each passing day.

Never could I have envisioned how strong my feelings would be when you took me into your arms, held my face in your hands and kissed me, ever so softly.

THINKING OF YOU ALWAYS

hinking of you always.

You have brought me so much joy and opened up my heart so much that the thought of never finding you is incomprehensible.

I think about the future, being with you and having a life with you makes everything so clear.

It's like the final piece of the puzzle in my life.

I never could have imagined my future could look so bright as it looks right now.

Please take my hand and lead me to your wonderful paradise because where you go I will follow.

You're my angel from above who has captured both my heart and soul and I'll always love you.

PART III
NEW BEGINNINGS

BEAUTY ALL AROUND US

Beautiful morning. With every new day there are new and beautiful things to be able to see and cherish.

Glorious morning.

Life is a beautiful thing. Welcome to the world little one.

Pretty bird up in the tree watching over everything.

Pretty among the branches and flowers.

Stormy skies. Beautiful flowering trees against the darkened skies.

Looking pretty.

Pink flowers in bloom. Spring is here.

Vulture flying overhead. Searching for remains.

Beautiful in flight.

Beautiful sight to behold. Sitting pretty in the branches.

Weathered bones.

Beautiful bare branches.

Beautiful in flight.

Two of a kind just hanging out.

Spreading its wings and on a mission up in the beautiful skies today.

On the lookout.

Traveling over.

Looking up into the beautiful bare branches.

Taking a break.

Beautiful bare tree branches.

Birds in flight.

Beauty above.

Perched on the rooftop.

An old swing.

Like two peas in a pod. Just enjoying the morning together.

Cold outside.

Beautiful skies.

Woodpecker soaring in the sky.

Cloudy morning.

All snuggled up for a wonderful night.

Hanging out on a cold morning.

Looking down from the branches.

Beautiful, cloudy day.

Glorious morning.

Bunny on the run.

Gorgeous clouds with birds flying over.

Beautiful greenery.

Sun peeking through on an early morning.

Doves hanging out.

High up in the trees looking down on the world below.

Beautiful cloud coverage.

Beauty in the trees.

Fog along the horizon this morning.

Beautiful start to the day.

Happy dog rolling in the winter snow.

A winter wonderland.

Little snow covered house. Just waiting for new occupants when spring sets in.

Pretty bird.

Storm brewing.

Darkened skies.

Early morning.

Glorious skies at night.

Fun for the holidays.

Sun peeking out from along the horizon.

Beautiful moon at night filtering through the branches.

Pretty pink tree flowers.

Sitting pretty.

It's a beautiful fall morning.

I'm ready for an adventure.

Half a moon tonight.

Fall is among us. Beautiful colors.

Nature is beautiful.

Flower budding.

Mushroom in the grass.

Above the clouds. Beautiful!

Flying high.

Having fun on the trail.

Just hanging out together.

Another beautiful sunset.

Just hanging around.

Out in the country enjoying what nature has to offer me.

Beautiful pine tree.

Just saying hi!

Beauty is all around us.

Moth in action.

Beautiful in orange.

Pretty in pink.

Glorious red.

Pretty pink flower in bloom.

Spring has sprung.

Just thought I would hop by to say hello.

My good boy. My best friend Teddy and I.

The life of a dog.

Pretty in purple.

Red roses.

Pretty in purple.

Tiny baby saved.

Cloudy morning.

Pretty flowers in the trees.

Beauty in the branches.

Beautiful trees.

Life is beautiful!

Who, me?

A bumblebee in action collecting pollen.

Beautiful in spring.

Pretty yellow.

Beautiful capture of a colorful butterfly.

Pretty purple flower.

Nature at its finest.

Trees in bloom.

Purple colors.

Vibrant crabapple tree in bloom.

An old, but beautiful tree.

I'm just gonna hang out here for a moment.

Just curious about this snow covered bush.

A beautiful snow covered morning to wake up to.

Snow covered face.

It's a happy day.

The world of a ladybug.

A gorgeous morning here.

Budding flower.

Marigolds in bloom.

Cloudy, yet beautiful day.

Pretty, colorful flowers.

Beautiful blue butterfly.

Amazing pic of a dragonfly perched for a while.

Pretty in yellow.

Beautiful.

Nature's own blessing.

White is beautiful.

Cute bunnies gathering.

Just stopping for a bit.

What are you?

A quiet time out on the waters.

Majestic waterfall scene.

Blooming flowers.

Beautiful sunlight filtering down through the branches.

A beautiful butterfly captured.

Let's just rest for a while.

Tiny little baby.

A beautiful morning with the sun filtering through the branches.

A beautiful and cloudy morning.

Pretty in white.

Home grown.

Beautiful scenery.

Harvest time.

What do you smell?

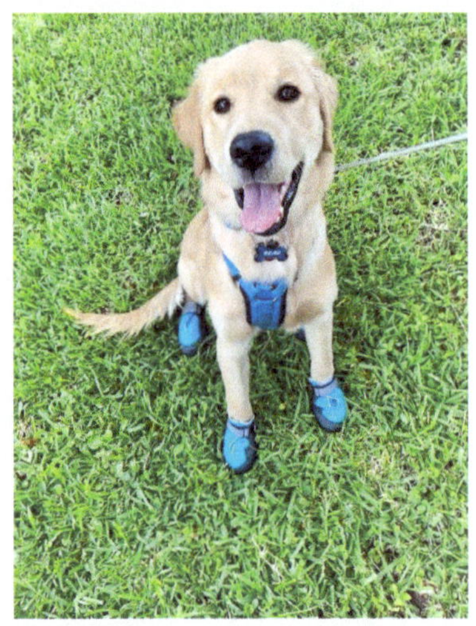

Look at me in my blue shoes.

Pretty colors.

Ready for my nap.

Starfish on the beach.

Pretty flowers.

Call me beautiful.

A moment in time.

Home grown strawberries.

Enjoying the day!

Yeah, I can lift this. No problem.

Strawberry flowers.

A little baby bunny.

Pretty and pink in the trees.

Up and away.

Silly girl.

Flowering trees in the spring.

A walk along the beach in the evening.

Little critter.

An old and beautiful tree.

Blackberries in season.

Can I see Santa too?

Creepy crawler.

Me and my best friend.

Spooky morning.

Mr. Scarecrow.

Yeah, I'm cute and I know it!

What's happening over there?

Chilling.

On the watch.

Wanna play?

Looking cute.

Looking cute.

My little munchkin.

A day on the harbor.

Beautiful day on the water.

Juicy, homegrown grapes.

Beautiful flowers.

Cats investigating.

Pirates at sea.

We don't want a bath.

Pretty butterfly resting.

Geese on the move.

Signs of spring.

ABOUT THE AUTHOR

I am a passionate writer who loves to weave together themes of nature and love in my work.

As an avid photographer and gardener, I find endless inspiration in the beauty of the natural world and the joy of life.

I reside in Delaware, where I cherish spending time with my two grown children and embrace every new experience with enthusiasm and curiosity.

My deep appreciation for animals and the environment is reflected in both my writing and my daily life.

Angelica Oliver

www.ingramcontent.com/pod-product-compliance
Lightning Source LLC
Chambersburg PA
CBHW040037150726
48196CB00041B/917